FRESH PACK OF SMOKES

To Victoria,
Best Wishes,

FRESH
PACK OF
SMOKES

CASSANDRA BLANCHARD

NIGHTWOOD EDITIONS

2019

Nightwood Editions
P.O. Box 1779, Gibsons, BC, VON 1V0, Canada
www.nightwoodeditions.com

EDITOR: Amber McMillan
COVER DESIGN: Angela Yen
TYPOGRAPHY: Carleton Wilson

Canada

Canada Council   Conseil des Arts
for the Arts   du Canada

BRITISH COLUMBIA
ARTS COUNCIL
An agency of the Province of British Columbia

Nightwood Editions acknowledges the support of the Canada Council for the Arts,
which last year invested $153 million to bring the arts to Canadians throughout the country.
Nous remercions le Conseil des arts du Canada de son soutien. L'an dernier, le Conseil
a investi 153 millions de dollars pour mettre de l'art dans la vie des Canadiennes et des
Canadiens de tout le pays. We also gratefully acknowledge financial support from
the Government of Canada and from the Province of British Columbia through
the BC Arts Council and the Book Publishing Tax Credit.

This book has been produced on 100% post-consumer recycled, ancient-forest-free paper,
processed chlorine-free and printed with vegetable-based dyes.

Printed and bound in Canada.

LIBRARY AND ARCHIVES CANADA CATALOGUING IN PUBLICATION

Blanchard, Cassandra, 1987-, author
Fresh pack of smokes / Cassandra Blanchard.

Poems.
Issued in print and electronic formats.
ISBN 978-0-88971-352-9 (softcover).--ISBN 978-0-88971-142-6 (ebook)

I. Title.

PS8603.L35314F74 2019   C811'.6   C2018-904790-9
                                        C2018-904791-7

for my family

Contents

PART ONE

PART TWO

PART THREE

There is a silence where hath been no sound,
There is a silence where no sound may be,
In the cold grave—under the deep deep sea

– Thomas Hood

Part One

XXX

I must have turned a thousand tricks over those six years, you name it I've done it, the perfect whore, young-looking so the men buzzed around me like bees on honey, you have no idea how many men see working girls for a quick blow job in the car after work before going home or taxi drivers or stockbrokers, all kinds like the author of children's books or the man who was a politician in Native self-government or probably your boyfriend or husband, there are the real cold mean ones and the okay ones who were not that bad and I mostly had middle-aged married white men and I guarantee that you know someone who has paid for sex; once I did a blow job where he blew his load in exactly three seconds or the vampire-looking dude with a foot-long boner that made me almost piss myself, but it's always been strictly business, I've been around the block for sure. At a Québécois rehab centre, there was the gender rule, *no breaking gender*, as in no fucking with either gender and of course I broke that rule multiple times, at night when everyone was asleep I would slide into bed with my woman and quietly make her cum, I couldn't not do it and it didn't help when a chick would get a crush on me, I guess I had to break the rules, it felt so good to be bad—I've never even been on a date before, it has always been straight to screwing, I guess it would be nice to go out for dinner rather than sleeping with some-one in secret, for two years we were together, the violent psycho and me, the pushover, but damn we clicked in the sack and everywhere too like in a semi or on the bus or outside, the only time we got along was when we were fucking, this bitch was a sociopath, I swear her eyes had nothing behind them but even though I was in danger around her, she made me feel safe and made me feel like I was losing the hamster wheel race, seriously though, I've had enough to last me three thousand years and that's nothing to be happy about, being for sale ain't nothing to be proud of.

BEGINNINGS

In the beginning I had no real knowledge of drugs as they came into my life through a series of bad decisions and being in the wrong place at the wrong time—I look back and think of how naive I was; it all started with a panhandler, her name was Anna and I always gave her change and one day I sat beside her and that became a routine until someone else came by and she was a snaky manipulative thing called Jane. Soon we started hanging out and she cut up a line of crystal meth for us, I was a little drunk and snorted that up rather quickly as I thought it was crushed ecstasy, not jib, and the next couple days were spent snorting and drinking and hallucinating green army men on the mountains, I never smoked crack until a few months later as I realized that meth was destroying me like how jib was coming out of my pores or seeing shadow beings or rotting my mouth, so when a friend lit the pipe for me I was stupid and glad for it as the high was better even though I wanted more as soon as possible, so there it was the beginning of the long spiral down, sometimes I look back and think how dumb I was and how thorough this addiction was and that being too trusting and believing in the good in people was my downfall.

THE FUZZ

I've had my share of dealing with the police and I've noticed things over the years, like the fact that female cops are stricter than males, it seems that they're trying to prove something cuz they're women and don't want to seem weak, they search people more too, I admit if I see a cop nowadays my heart does a tiny little jump cuz for so long I kept six and tried to avoid them as much as possible, and how funny it was when cops walking will clear a block faster than anything—like a scattering of rats—but the most intense encounter I've had with the fuzz was when I threw knives at them wanting them to shoot me but they didn't and instead I got tackled so violently I limped for the next couple months, some are not that bad though like the woman cop that carries around a Ziploc bag of cigarettes who gave me and my friend a smoke instead of telling us to clear out or the cop who talked to me about rehab and treatment or the cop who let me go a few times, of course there are the pricks and cunts who walk around reeking of arrogance and riding a power trip with their flashlights and gloves and handcuffs—once when I was very green and got searched and the cop took my pipe and told me I could be arrested especially if there was lots of resin and then he gave it back to me and told me he was trying to school me and to get lost, needless to say I was small potatoes to him, it's a contradiction because it's great not having them around but having them around gives a feeling of protection what with all those nasty predators stalking about.

PEOPLE

Of course this place is full of goofs and predators and victims and murderers and it plays by the rules of money and drugs and sex and you will meet the worst of the worst and learn how cold hearts can be, but there are also those who still have humanity and it's those people I remember the most, like those who opened their rooms for me when I was cold and messed up or the man who didn't even get mad when I puked inside his car or those who told me their heart-breaking life stories and who walked always on a sharp edge living in the darkness and rain, women who had children they barely saw, or weren't allowed to see, and families torn apart by addiction, this thing called life, this sadness carried through time; these people will be forgotten and will disappear and fade away and their kindness will go into shadows.

CARL ROOMS

She smiled a smile that was all gums, apparently she had the shit kicked out of her and all her upper teeth were shattered and she had to get them all taken out—she was so young it was strange that her mouth looked like an old woman's and even though I forget her name I'll never forget her gums, we were in Carl Rooms which was a level better than all those bed bug–infested piece of shit hotels; Tecia told me how the janitors in Carl Rooms would sometimes open the tenants' rooms, those fuckers were like cockroaches roaming around in the hallways, or the two French goofballs who would use the ladies' washroom and clog it with shit and piss making the chick who cleaned them gag from the stink of it, you have the pregnant dealer who smoked rock and drank Fireball Cinnamon Whisky or the chick who very carefully injected heroin into her neck and spent the next half hour nodding on the floor; I hear stories sometimes told to me, like a son who shoots his uncle in the head and predators hurting daughters in order to get back at the mothers and twenty-two-year-olds who look like they're sixty and especially unfriendly eyes that watch from the shadows.

TALES

One night in Oppenheimer Park, Dan asked me to shit-kick this chick in the face as she owed money and I said *no* because I didn't know who she was and I wasn't about to play with fire so he sat on the bench then stood up and did a flying kick twice to her chin and she convulsed and passed out he said he didn't want to spill blood because she had HIV, after a few weeks the woman told me she didn't remember anything and that pissed Dan off; once I sold drugs for a Mexican who could break bats and I was ten dollars short so he smacked me twice on the street and later I got so bloody drunk I slept with him and couldn't believe I did that, I will never sell drugs for someone again because it's like being handcuffed, when I first met Jay we got into a screaming match over something I don't remember, we became great friends because I helped him out and he helped me out and he told me that not wanting to sleep with him made him want to try even more but one time a white guy—he was one of those men who liked big black cocks—it was like ring around the rosy as I sucked the white guy's cock and the white guy was sucking the black guy's cock and I found the whole thing rather strange and I thought how people come down here to procure the services of young girls or young boys or cheap women or black guys or females that look young; I had a violent encounter with a former lover, she is so messed up and cruel though she used to treat me well but that went away when she found out how much of a cash cow I am and she no longer respected me and all we did was fight and get kicked out of every place we tried to stay and then after I came out of jail we only saw each other sometimes and the last time we met I called her a bitch and she put her hand on my throat and was very close to breaking my face with her punch when I yelled out, *DO IT! DO IT! I WANT YOU TO DO IT!* and her eyes changed and she didn't punch me because I gave her psychosis, I know how her mind works, being high on crack makes it easier to be used for cash, all the faces are just a series of blurs with no names and no identities, all I want is cash, I know how to squeeze money out of men they are so simple and yet so dangerous, you see I didn't care that much and still don't really care. That might not be normal.

THE ASTORIA

The Astoria is the hotel I was most afraid of and it isn't what I saw or heard or touched, it was what I did not see or hear, the silence was terrifying and I knew the walls had eyes and ears and rooms with people who seemed to never come out, once or twice I rented a room and once I was in someone's room and both times I felt there was something frightening outside in the halls, there was a liquor store and a bar at the hotel and there was always some kind of show happening but it was the hotel itself that creeped the bejesus out of me and the East Indians who manned the desk, who knows who the fuck they were; I felt like there were ghosts in there.

PARTNERS

Sometimes I would partner up with another addict in our endless quest for drugs, I forget her name but I hung with this one woman for a few days and we would take turns buying crack, and also heroin for her, and we would sit somewhere and do dope, when we had to sleep we stayed at her friend's place and in the morning he gave us money in exchange for a date and we were on the hunt again, however eventually we parted ways and I was glad cuz hanging with junkies was kind of annoying with all the nodding out and the needles and the constant search for heroin to avoid being sick; there were times I would share my dope cuz I would get stuck in the alley if I smoked rock alone, however sometimes I'd think the person I was with was secretly plotting against me, I just really didn't like using alone, I was hanging with this guy just as company, nothing else, and we were sitting in the park when cops came and they ran our names and it came up that I had a violent encounter with police so they left us alone but the guy was freaked out as he didn't like violence so that ended that and it went on like that, person to person, things didn't work out or they did, of course I sought out other people cuz I was lonely and isolated and needed to feel a connection.

BIOGRAPHIES

Candy's hair was her resumé, she was my street mom and she taught me how to behave in jail, taught me where the good places are on the street and who to avoid, she has many street kids as her children, she is the only person I truly respected in that world.

Taylor works out of the Sunwest, she told me people have different addictions and her addiction is money, sometimes she carries a bat with her to deal with the goofs and miscreants or people who disrespect the place, I have done dates in that hotel and I have to say it felt a little safer than doing shit in a car.

Tecia and Sandy are mother and child, it's strange seeing a parent smoke crack with their kid but this kind of thing happens here, they always let me seek shelter and I shared my stuff with them; Sandy has arthritis and needs methadone and is always in pain, Tecia has a psychopath for a boyfriend who stabbed her with a push stick, beats her up and is generally a prick.

CHARACTERS

This one girl was slender but strong and obviously wired off her fucking mind and this dealer paid her twenty bucks to knock out his worker who was hiding in the contact centre behind the Carnegie, she was obviously someone to be careful with and she packed one hell of a punch, and there was an older woman who people called Draco, she told me she was a dangerous person and could sense people's characters and that she trusted me with her keys which was cool but her room was a dump with mice running all over but it was better than outside in the rain, and Sarah was a pregnant lady who nevertheless still smoked crack and drank whisky and was a local dealer and often cuffed people so there was always someone who owed her money, she was pretty popular and was nice to me despite my feelings about women doing hard drugs while with child, and there was a white chick named Dina who defended my honour and punched out this Vietnamese guy and even spoke the language herself, she was a good person to have on your side and we would go on binges until no money was left but over time she grew more haggard as being on the streets sucks the life out of people, and black men down here are very confident and so pushy that they give me the creeps, there was always some black guy trying to get in my pants but Jay was different cuz he was a gentleman, and there was a chick named Gin who frequented the alley behind the Carnegie and wasn't someone you'd want to piss off, she was this short Native chick with a weathered face who howled like a wolf and tried to pick fights when she was drunk, and Shelly was a woman who you actually really did not want to tick off and she has fucked up those who did and I lived for a few months in the same house with her and we basically got along and even though she was tough she could not escape an ass whooping when she called the guy in the basement a "goof" and like I said before it was like someone poured a bucket of blood all over her.

SPANISH VILLA

It was a cheap and raggedy apartment building but it was affordable
and one day we were looking at a place there and I was very young
and it was just my sisters and my mom and I was alone looking at
one of the rooms when the landlord came up to me and put his hand
around my throat and whispered, "I don't believe you"—I was con-
fused and did not tell anyone until many years later and I remember
now the looks he would give me every time I saw him, when she had
a question or whatever, which really wasn't that often and today I'm
pretty sure he had done things to children.

JAIL

I was not prepared for the amount of waiting that occurs, I waited to be processed and waited to be transferred and waited in the wagon and waited in court and waited to eat and waited to be counted; everything slowed down to a set routine where time was measured, inmates were arrested for drugs and often their drug was heroin so unless they have methadone right away they get down sick and having a cellmate who is going through smack withdrawal sucks, my first cellmate managed to smuggle in crystal meth but she left after a couple days and I was glad cuz it's not the greatest to be in close quarters with a person on meth; I was going to be transferred to ACCW since my security risk was minimum so I waited in the holding cell for the sheriffs to frisk me and then waited in the wagon to go to the facility—what followed was the basic routine in which everyone is bored so the dramatics are elevated, I was lucky I was only there for four months but I felt sorry for the women headed to federal, like this one woman facing twenty-five or another charged with giving a man HIV—after lunch I always worked out and in the evenings lifted weights, during the day I shot hoops but I spent most hours sitting in the gazebo smoking cigarettes; when I was waiting to be released it felt like time was creeping by, as if seconds were minutes and minutes were hours and the world just slowed right down.

CAMP CUPCAKE

Detoxing in the cells, slowly the psychosis goes away but I was still sure there was someone in the toilet talking to me and I can definitely hear loud drips in the plumbing system, I swear my brain is swiss cheese; one good thing is in the North Van court cells they gave you McDonald's for lunch and I like to put French fries in my burger and I get a kick out of the woman sheriff who looks like Santa Claus with a mullet but I keep quiet and listen to the noises; before the cells, before jail, there was a lonely kid who wanted to die, who wanted not to live and so I ended up inside and met characters larger than life, fucked up, like the prison guard who called me stupid cuz I dropped a piece of paper or Red who kept on entering the country illegally to see her kids or the mental woman whom everyone in jail hated or the two East Indian women who tortured someone, or so they say; ACCW is called "Camp Cupcake" cuz it's so easy to do your time there plus it isn't federal—federal is a whole different ball game—and all that estrogen in one place, women are fucking in the bathrooms and anywhere else they can try and take away the loneliness.

It's hard to explain what it's like to have your freedom taken away, how scared you are, a world all its own, a whole different reality; I learned that if you act like a bitch, you'll be treated as such.

WOMEN

I would have to say that women are insidious, women play mind games and are turncoats and when they're hardened, they're more dangerous than men and have potential for violence and a dog's ability to sniff out weaknesses, and women never forget, they'll hold a grudge to the end of time, they are masters of psychological warfare and will enslave and hold hostage without shedding blood, these women are usually a bit older and have been hooked on narcotics for years and their entire lives revolve around using and dealing drugs, they will be your best friend until the money is gone and then they'll be gone too, some are solid but it's best not to make too many friends because in the end you're nobody's buddy.

DRAMATIS PERSONAE

Suzy bullshitted the wrong bitch and had her orbital broken so she walks around looking like a piece of rotten meat and was lucky she didn't end up in a coffin, she takes advantage of weak girls and tricks them into getting cuffed so they're fucked and stuck while she licks her chops in the alley behind the Patricia Hotel in the freezing cold, digging her own hole; I watch her from Carl Rooms and realize I hope for her downfall, another one, I'll call her Kay, bears scars from living day-to-day getting high and forgetting how to cry, she says anger grips her all the time, she lost people because of it, not really giving a shit, for a dense moment we meet and touch and I taste her, finger-fuck her senseless, until she stops trembling and though this is a brief fling, I'll never forget Kay who down there she will always stay; Sunny tells me how heroin has stolen her emotions as she sticks the syringe in with ease, her mouth hanging open, she is a lifelong dope fiend, everything inside her is dead.

MAPLE RIDGE

Somehow we ended up in Maple Ridge where we stayed for a week or so at this dude's place and then went out for days hunting money for drugs while Kim got almost-daily Western Union money from her sugar daddy, our combined drug habits needed more cash so I did what she trained me to do and that was servicing men for money and I remember hustling on this block called North Road late at night and this one guy who I had a date with never picked up a girl before so he was nervous and generous with money, I could state any price and I have to admit I felt sorry for the bloke, he looked like he was going to piss himself, this block on North Road was dark and dangerous and the business was pretty good, I didn't think too much about danger cuz if I did I would not be able to do this shit and if I was not able to do this shit then I would be punished and pressured to get back into it and it was guaranteed money which was the most important thing, it was like drugs were more important than my life, so this one dude picked me up and I actually preferred his company over Kayla's and so I spent time with him, he was an okay guy but cuz of my misplaced sense of loyalty I called Kayla in front of him and he told me I sounded like I was afraid of her and he didn't want to become part of it so I left and went back doing the same old bull-shit; there was a crack house in Maple Ridge we frequented for a bit run by a scary dude named Dodd who was pretty decent to me and I met this woman there who hustled as well and she was disturbed by how young I was and that I was doing this shit and other people were often disturbed that Kayla, who supposedly loved me, would let me do something like sell myself to help feed our expensive hab-its, but in the end everything is all about money.

MARKET AND METAL

On Hastings there's a black market of sorts that goes on for a block where one can find things like steaks and porn and clothes, people have their shopping carts full of junk and dealers hustle the crowd, Glen and Kim and I used to drive a large old van around scrounging for food in the back lot of the Superstore and then selling it on the street, this block is crowded and when police walk the beat the crowd disperses fast like mice and then regroups, we also used our van to collect metal and sell it at the junkyard and if you collect enough you can get quite a bit of money, those old radiators are good to scrap, once a big truck went by and a chicken fell out and sat there in the middle of the road and for a minute I thought I was seeing things cuz it came out of nowhere and it was one of those poultry who can't walk anymore and two seconds later a dude took the chicken, probably to sell it in Chinatown I don't know, but I felt sorry for that chicken and I would have carried it to the SPCA but the man was quicker than me so that's how it goes.

THE DRUNK TANK

It started with too much crack, soon I was hearing voices through the electrical lines and I followed their arguments for hours, time was non-existent and I ended up downtown in the rain shuffling along the curb, I was occupying a place in between realities and on one hand a man was trying to drag me into the alley and on the other hand a woman was annoyed because I was attracting too much heat and I was because the next thing I knew I was in St. Paul's, the nurses wrapping me in blankets trying to warm me but I got scared cuz I didn't know I had gone to a hospital, all I knew was people were touching me and soon the nurse's kindness turned to anger and she threw me out on the street; somehow I made it across the road and passed out on the flower bed outside 7-Eleven, the cops came and didn't believe that my name was my name until they ran it through the system, I was put in the drunk tank with two tough women for an hour or so before they let me go and I went down the street to Princess and curled up between a pay phone and some stairs; I called my parents and waited for them to pick me up cuz they still helped me even during the times when I was truly screwed up.

SHELTER

For a while Kayla and I stayed at a house with other drug addicts owned by an old man with a serious hoarding problem, one guy named Hal lived in the basement and spent most of his days watching the AMC channel and there was a man who lived in the room beside him and who stunk like garbage and took bottles to the depot but I don't remember his name, there was Sally on the main floor who was a drug dealer and rather dangerous and there was Ted who collected food found in the back lots of grocery stores and then sold it on Hastings, Kayla and I lived on the top floor in an attic-style room that had a bed and table and that was where we did drugs and all of us generally got along, I was mostly high, I don't remember if we went to the North Van shelter first or the shelter by the hospital but I do know we met different people like the woman at the shelter with the two dogs or the guy in North Van who was addicted to Percocets or the few people who let us in at night, anyway we were trying to avoid sleeping on the streets which was something we sometimes did whenever we were between places, it was a situation where sleeping safely was a bonus so Kayla often stayed awake for a week at a time, either drunk or high, or blasted with Valium or often all three and I have to say I got worried when she was sleep deprived cuz she would smoke gigantic crack tokes which made me fear her heart would burst; once she gave Ted a huge toke and a couple minutes later barricaded the door cuz she thought bad people were coming to get us or when this young dude we hung out with for a while received a toke from Kayla and tore his shirt off or when she did it to me and I'd think we would be killed by men with knives—this constant need to be high became more important than having places to stay though we were often lucky enough to find somewhere to briefly inhabit until we fucked it up again.

PERFUME

Walk down turn right and follow the odour of shit and piss behind Carnegie where low-level dealers and rats roughly the size of small cats scurry by the overflowing garbage dumpsters, some roaming addicts rip-roaring high and stuck in the hole in the wall scared of the blue cruisers and their rubber-glove searches, walk through the scary empty corridors of the Astoria Hotel, a place where bad things happen but nobody ever seems to be around, with dried blood stains on old mattresses infested with bed bugs, beside it the small liquor store where 24/7 alcoholics lurk while sipping Listerine, crack pipes burn lips so toxic that spiders appear out of nowhere and crawl all over skin and floors and pieces of Brillo get stuck in lungs; some twirl around in the alley demanding free cigarettes from passersby, some are on hands and knees picking at wax or sometimes it's like snipers are in the buildings with trained guns and black helmets, smell the street, how it's an entity unto itself like cold concrete vessels with dirty puddles and scary people who'll fuck you over and fuck you up, that block-long street market with hustlers and dealers and scrapers and that smell that permeates the air; down here nothing is fair, it's a circus with old ghosts walking the alleys as those predators tread lightly and silently behind the innocent.

VGH

Instead of pumping my stomach they make me drink a cup of charcoal as they realize the pills have formed a ball and will slowly turn my blood toxic so then I'm wheeled into the psych ward and spend a few hours sweating while my nose drips blood all over the bed and wall; I wake up with a bag of fluids hooked up to my arm and alone in a cell-like room with a grey metal toilet as the nurse watches me like a hawk; I broke into my family home and swallowed a bunch of Aspirin and like a chicken decided I didn't want to die and so they came for me, in the hospital I went, the doctors act like they've seen this so many times before; the other patients are curious like a girl who thinks she's pregnant with Jesus and the schizoid who follows me around while blushing which is kind of cute; I'm here in this ward for days and my mind turns to normal for a while and it's scary, more scary than living on the edge, and as soon as I'm free from this ward I score and I get so fucking high that I know for sure there are dead people in the air ducts; I guess this attempt at suicide gave me a vacation from life for a bit and though I've hurt those who love me, I'm grateful for the pause.

STARS

Instead of calling the ambulance they dumped his body on some-one's lawn, my father had overdosed on heroin and his so-called friends were too afraid of the police to try and save his life and so the cops came to our house and because we were children they gave teddy bears to us, however I was asleep when the officers came so I woke up to my sister crying and she said *he passed away* and I thought he fell in a ditch, passing away like falling, and so I went to my mother who was in the shower crying and she told me he was dead and I understood; my memories are there but there are not so many of them and some of them I would rather not remember like the alcohol he was dependent on and the violence that came with it; he was troubled but he loved us, I look up at the sky and to me he is a lone star in the ever darkening cosmos.

Part Two

VARIETIES

The four of them drove around the Woodbine in a white sedan looking for girls stupid enough to get in the vehicle with them while a man in a green van asked every girl if they do anal, I heard that a second Indo hid in the back; there were also semi trucks driven by truckers who regularly picked up chicks, then you have the cheap-ass taxi drivers who pick up on Campbell Street, cover the camera in their cars; these are some examples of men who vary but what they all have in common is that they are weak when you know how to reduce them to jelly; a lot of them are the same, some have the weirdest fantasies you would never know by looking at them, like this one guy loved the thought of a chick slurping up his bowl of cum, with a spoon of course, I didn't do shit like that as I felt sick even thinking about it; there are a lot of trans sex workers down here as well like this six-foot-four black lady with long dreads and sharp high heels—she defiantly owned it—and men walking the block looking for boys to hook up with and guys driving around the block all over Hastings jerking off with no pants on, once this chick threw a rock at one of these voyeurs; this one man was deaf and mute and drove a special car to work with his special condition, I have to say at first I thought what the hell was I doing with someone like that but he was trying so hard to communicate it was pathetic in a kind of cute way—it is such an easy way to make fast cash—and having been hazed into it, it's something that I did very simply and eventually without much emotion.

BATTLES

I am not a very good fighter, I've doled out a couple weak fists but I've mostly had my ass beat, I think the worst part of being kicked in the face is the back of your head slamming into the wall, and there is so much blood—you swallow the chunks like dark red liver; I was living in this place and one night the woman who lived below walked up the stairs and came into our room, she had been beaten to the point where it looked like someone poured a bucket of blood on her like I said, apparently she called someone a "goof," you never call someone that unless you're ready to fight, so I woke up in the worst way when someone was toying around with mace and accidently sprayed me in the face, I fell off the bed and slammed against the wall; the woman stuck a pipe in my mouth and gave me a hoot to forget that I couldn't breathe, a sort of Band-Aid I guess; these are battles I wish I could forget but they stay like the scars on my body that I sometimes still pick at and open.

FEAR

Many times when I smoked crack I felt a very specific kind of fear, it was like a good part of my high was this feeling of dread and being scared that someone would kill me and this would go on until my high faded and then all I felt was longing for another toke and then it would come back and I would fear that I was being set up and that I was being surrounded, this conspiracy psychosis gave me a rush and I often hallucinated police lights on every vehicle driving by which didn't make the paranoia any better and I would distrust anyone I was with or anyone who was around me and I would hide my pipe; when done right I smoked dope in the middle of the day walking down the street, I did this by using copper pipe fittings and one of those skinny hoses that I fastened on the pipe where I put the Brillo and I would put the hose up through my sleeve and the end of it just a little out of my collar where I could put my mouth on it easily, I would light the thing with a torch lighter while holding the pipe just out of my sleeve and when I was done I tucked it away; I did this after seeing Kayla do it and doing tokes like that gave me adrenaline and of course the insistent feeling that I was going to die or be killed by persons unknown and when I'm down again I think about how stupid it was that I was hooked on something that gave me so much fear as well as so much pleasure.

LOVE I

I thought it was love but really it was exploitation, it took me years to comprehend how much Kayla had damaged me and my soul and my sanity and especially my trust of other people—relationships that are based on drugs are never healthy, it's like a black peach, it looks good on the outside but once you bite it, it's all rotten on the inside; I went from being a partner to a cash cow to feed our drug habits and our desperation and rootlessness haunted us until there was no respect anymore, like a lone shoestring, the only thing that held us together was sex whether it was us making love or for men who paid me a lot of money for services—I remember the first time I ever turned a trick, I was nineteen and when a dealer asked for a blow job I said that I didn't do that kind of stuff and of course behind my back he asks Kayla if I would do it for a substantial amount of crack, she didn't ask me she told me and therefore I did it and that started an influx of dates. Once these exchanges began to be normal for us, the respect she had for me vanished and I was no longer a person but a means to get more money and drugs, violence came with it and it came slowly until she was head-butting me on the street or pulling my hair or scaring me with a hunting knife and I had to deal with her psychosis, which was unbearable; I am sure Kayla is cold inside, but she did make me feel warm and I loved her though I had every reason not to and I wonder now if she's dead or alive and if she is alive what her life is like and then I get angry because why should I care.

DIAL-A-DOPE

For a long time we used the dial-a-dope system instead of buying from hustlers on the street, it was a system that worked as it's better to be inside and high and not outside getting paranoid from all the potential trouble, and of course the cops, so we called the dealer and either he came in through the back door or someone got in the car and drove around the block to do the deal, the dial-a-dope dealers we did business with were mostly young Asian men with slick cars but not so slick as to bring attention and the dope itself was good, not the nasty meth-like crap you get on the block and it weighed proper wrapped in plastic, over time you built business relationships with these dealers and maybe once in a while you could cuff dope and they'd trust you to pay it back but I hated owing anybody anything, I'd rather go without rock than owe money and owing money to people like them wasn't smart, maybe on the street you could score pretty fast but there is always a risk of getting ripped off because that window of opportunity between the moment you have cash and the moment you get your dope is what goofs live for, so it was worth the wait for the dealers to take the time and drive to where you were and even though that wait can be torture, the moment you smoked that crack it was all good.

BEHAVIOUR

I learned how to fuck people over and take advantage of their feelings, like I managed to convince my friend to send me money, I got a couple hundred dollars off of this one couple and since sex work is all about squeezing money out of clients, I underwent an education in how to grind money off men in order to feed this habit that sucked the decency out of me, this habit that had thrown me into a dark and endless hole, I appealed to whatever was someone's weaknesses like playing the young helpless girl, or *the best blow job you'll ever get* for which I would receive a substantial tip, or straight out seducing passersby which is a lot easier than you think as I've done it countless times, or playing along with a fantasy like this guy who liked to be called "master" and who talked about his tiny penis with the utmost confidence, or after a date sometimes the man wants to hold hands while he drives me back; I was trained to get what I want from people and I was driven by selfishness in order to score drugs since that's the point of it all anyway isn't it, and I was surrounded by people who did the same damn thing over and over and who thrive off weakness, but before I was armed I was an object preyed upon by scare tactics and manipulation so I guess it's a twisted version of paying it forward but I managed to do my time without getting into a fight in fact I had friends but jail doesn't rehabilitate and soon after being released and rehabbed I was out again taking advantage of people and sometimes being taken advantage of myself.

PILLS, BOOZE AND WEED

Pills were something I usually didn't do, instead it was Kayla who would take lots of Valium for days on end and I liked her on that more than on crack cuz she was less controlling and was nicer, I took a couple pills once to come down from a binge and I fell asleep while walking and ran into trees and stumbled in the middle of the road and I woke up standing and was surrounded by police who were in a couple cars and on foot, there must have been six of them but they let me go, during the times that I drank it was to go all the way, no sipping just chugging it down til I was down drunk and many times I blacked out and woke up in strange places but I preferred crack to alcohol cuz booze made me more vulnerable; weed was never really my thing but Kayla smoked it to level things in her head and she became so much more calm, I wished she would smoke weed every day but those days were becoming far and few between, I feel like I needed something to give me some sort of sensation whether it was the first smoke of the day or cheap wine or rock, there was a need in me to alter my consciousness as much as possible.

LOVE II

I was in love with crack cocaine, so close, warming me when I was cold, just me and my rock, the ultimate loneliness of holding my pipe in my fist and not caring if I die, not caring if I live this sad lie, the shit I would do to score these little white pebbles of cocaine just boggles my mind but fuck it was all worth it when I inhaled that smoke and the dope hit my brain; like a cat I had nine lives, I should have died so many times and I feel like I broke up with my best friend who was closer to me than my own folks; I whisper softly and drink clear moonshine to forget the pain of leaving this love behind.

DON'T WORRY IT'S ONLY PSYCHOSIS

They hide in vents in gates in fences in cars and right behind me this is madness this is insanity, the telephone poles talk to me and tell me to walk around them exactly three times, there are strange connections in a very scary Wonderland and I am a very sad Alice and I whisper *it all goes down the drain*; I walk more and see those two dumbbells on Gore Street, Tweedledee and Tweedledum, then it gets worse cuz I'm answering myself now, an entire conversation, and we are arguing about whether we're being recorded because I can hear the playback.

STREETS AND AVENUES

Kingsway was where we spent a lot of time, the street is so long so it's never boring, for days I was on Joyce and Kingsway with Kayla making cash for drugs and since we didn't have a place of our own we stayed up for days on end, sometimes we got separated and I made money just for me and smoked crack in the bushes and those times we weren't together was always a relief but I blindly loved her and wanted her around cuz she protected me; there was a time Commercial Drive was rougher than it is now with addicts and criminals and gangs and for a short while I hung in the back alleys with a woman who introduced me to meth, I was so naive I bought her crack while I did crystal, on Kingsway there's the Cassandra Hotel where we spent a couple days with a decent enough guy who never asked for anything in return and it was nice to be inside after spending a while on the street, for days we were stuck in Maple Ridge and I did my business on North Road where it was dark and scary, I did it because I didn't care anymore what could happen to me on those roads; once we collected Kayla's welfare check in Kits and spent the whole day walking through the alleys doing dope which made me paranoid we were going to get arrested while loitering in this nice neighbourhood; we were walking around on Main Street close to Mount Saint Joseph Hospital and in the alley we found two hundred dollars on the ground so fuck the sugar daddy we got a half ball of rock and some cigarettes and we continued roaming, later on I got to know skid row better and found that it was more convenient than other places as there was everything you wanted, you just had to have the money; I've been all over Vancouver and every one of these places has a seedy underbelly to get lost in.

LOVE III

Down here there are situations where parents and offspring both use narcotics, one woman would tell her son to turn around so he wouldn't see her smoke rock and you could feel the shame radiating from her, and a mother and daughter lived down the hall from each other at Carl Rooms and regularly smoked crack together, both dealt together, both fought each other and both looked out for one another and before getting housing they lived in alleys and they have gone through things that are unbelievable and dark and I never knew how I felt about these families, like I couldn't imagine doing drugs in front of my mom, even the thought of drinking in front of her makes me very uncomfortable, but it's very easy to judge these women and to say how bad they are but only they know the reasons for their actions and why things turned out the way they did, it doesn't mean they don't love each other.

FOOD

It's very important to eat when you use a lot of drugs regularly, this was something I had trouble with as dope took away my appetite and I would go days without food and then I would vomit up the food when I did remember to eat like this one time I made myself eat a bowl of soup and a cup of milk and then I puked my guts out and soon after that I coughed up green bile because there was nothing in my stomach; one cannot starve in Vancouver as there are numerous places that give out free food and most people take advantage of these services but I became dope-simple and ignored the demands of my body and so I suffered when I finally tried to sleep as I twitched a lot and hallucinated spiders in my hair, crawling all over my arms and it took a long time until I settled enough to slip into sleep and then I would be tormented by twisted dreams.

TRIPS

Behind the Patricia Hotel is an alley with a couple holes in the wall and smelling like chicken and for a half-hour I could not bring myself to walk away, I was stuck in that alley thinking that the army had snipers in the windows of the buildings lining that lane, I thought that the snipers had their crosshairs on me and if I moved I would get shot, I actually hallucinated the barrels of their guns pointing at me, damn I must have hid behind that hotel for hours, the alley behind the Carnegie is a sketchy place that smells like hell and is full of tweekers and big rats and sometimes cops on horses, with dealers wheeling and dealing, with the odd spark of violence, it's so easy to get stuck in that place all day, all night with some getting jacked by cops and some getting shit-kicked for whatever offense and street-level dealers doing what they do, the block opposite Oppenheimer Park is a shitty little place with an alley parallel to it and it is full of small-time dealers practically in a line like a row of ducks hustling and twitching, the higher-level dealer named Fast supervised the business, he was a big dude you wouldn't want to fuck with and woe to those who do; the alley off Abbott Street is another piece-of-crap place in the back of a club smelling like wet old shit piss and garbage and again one can get too rip-roaring high and become stuck in that lane for a substantial amount of time all paranoid about cops and getting busted by undercovers, do a hit and become unable to move, every which way is danger—real or imagined—that church on the corner of Gore and East Hastings is mostly full of men and winos hang out in front at the bus stop and cops are there on a regular basis for whatever reason and those drunks sit there and watch the street opposite them where deals are made and drama goes down like a fucked-up reality show, they don't even need a TV.

LOVE IV

I was smoking heroin in the alley behind the Sunwest Hotel and it took me on a bender as me and this chick rode around in a van with a Russian driver going somewhere I don't know, I must have looked pitiful cuz a guy drove by and stopped to give me twenty bucks, he saw me massaging my blistered feet, and somehow I ended up in this woman's place drinking beer and smoking crack but I felt so bad cuz I was nodding out the whole time and I thought that was pretty rude as I passed out on her couch and proceeded to have the weirdest, most fucked-up dreams of my life, then I was suddenly awoken and the whole thing began again, my body was so tired and my mind was like a broken toaster—this heroin was a roller coaster, it felt so good and it was even better if you put a little crack on the pipe, it was like coming in and out of reality and I only remember bits and pieces of that night and how it was so easy to fall in love with smack.

HALLUCINATE

Many times I experienced cocaine psychosis in which I would hallucinate spiders and black worms—I dreaded it so much—spiders as big as tarantulas would crawl all over my arms and worms would twist around in my hair, I could feel them coming out of my pores and my body would shiver and twitch; on the first days of detox I would go through this terrible experience and again when I had to sleep after a bender, I would hallucinate when I took a massive hit of crack too like when I saw a man walking around with an axe and I got so scared, I freaked out the people I was with, right the fuck out, or I would see faces coming out of the shadows and snakes slithering in my pipe and the only thing that took the edge off all these hallucinations was if I got really drunk; I would always see these spiders after staying up for days using and not eating or drinking as much as I wanted, it was my body's way of telling me to stop or else I would lose my sanity and fuck man sometimes I think I did.

COPPER

With the angle of her movements she cuts me to the quick, I smell my blood, maybe I'll find the iron in her body, metal on my tongue—copper tastes like this—each beat beating my heart, I want to bite her thigh to feel alive and to trace the track marks that scare me so much—in all probability she'll die soon living this life, some anonymous tragedy where no one cares.

LOVE V

You are like an angel from God Tecia said as I do what few did which was to sit and listen to her story between hits of the crack pipe, sitting in the same spot for hours she says she loves me and that God sent me to her and the only thing I do is shut the fuck up and listen to her heartbreaking stories like how her son shot her brother in the head or how her boyfriend stabbed her with a push stick and smacks her around or how she was homeless and smoked rock with her daughter; I don't know why but this happened to me a lot, I would just listen and these women would pour their hearts out, every time I relapsed I would pop in on the crying woman and her daughter, I was guaranteed to stay safe and not get beaten up or robbed and Tecia would talk to me about her many lives, so the downside of quitting drugs is that I have to quit everyone as well, like I must ignore my heart strings, to give them up so it's better not to let others get under your skin, it's better not to make friends and it's especially wise not to care about anyone like how I grew to care about Tecia and her daughter.

TARGETS

She used to be a legal secretary and now after smoking so much dope she can't even talk right, nobody knows what she's trying to say and nobody makes an effort to so she gets taken advantage of—she let some guy fuck her in the ass for five bucks at the Sunwest—she shows up with this guy, who probably couldn't believe how cheap this nut job was, and she's told by management not to take the furniture apart again or she'll get kicked out; I've seen her walking drunk, talking nonsense and my friend whispers to me that it's all an act and that this crazy woman is getting the last laugh but I doubt it cuz it's obvious her brain is mush; this other woman wore a wool toque and a trench coat, shuffling around and talking to herself, every time I saw her I went the opposite way cuz there was a hint of hostility in her mumbling and I felt her demeanour was rather angry, I'd seen her on a bus before where she was having a conversation with herself and everyone was quiet until a man started telling her to shut up but she didn't as it probably didn't register, she would drag her feet around the streets looking for a small-time dealer since she usually only had three or five bucks for a tiny rock; there are so many women like this, crippled by disease and dope and mental illness, constantly targeted by those who prey on the weak, women whose humanity is consistently stripped until they are naked with no armour.

HOW GOOFS GET KILLED

I was in the Vancouver holding cells eating my brown-bag lunch of a bologna sandwich and a box of juice while the cell began to fill up with women either dressed in prison greys or street clothes, it was a rather large cell and it had a long bench so most of the women sat on that or on the floor against the wall, I sat in the corner facing out so I could see what goes on and so that nobody was behind me—it was an old habit that has taken a while to break, when one is incarcerated you go through a lot of waiting and whether that waiting is peaceful depends on who you are sharing the space with—and there was one woman who disrupted the atmosphere, she began to ask each woman why and how they ended up being locked up, it was obvious she wasn't playing with a full deck and didn't know that it was taboo to go around asking people why they're in jail cuz if they want you to know they'll tell you, though it was most likely that a lot of these women were arrested for drugs as some were still high; during questioning this one woman jumped up and shouted that she spent four years at FVI and all these women in greys told her acting like that is how goofs get killed, well that shut her up right quick and I did feel sorry for her but hey you got to learn somehow and almost getting stomped on probably taught her to mind her own business.

LONELY MEN

There are these men who are so lonely they feel the need to make friends when all you want is a quick and easy business deal, these men are so pathetic that I feel sorry for them as they hold my hand and talk about their day or try to kiss or cuddle imagining I'm their wife or something, however fulfilling fantasies was what I did for drug money so I held their hands while they drove around and engaged in affectionate conversation and smoked the cigarettes they gave me and ate the food they offered me; with these kind of guys, getting tips is practically guaranteed and even better was getting them to become regulars as I only had to accept the affection they gave which was strangely harder to do than it being strictly business; these men are pretty vanilla and aren't into pain or humiliation and are all in all pretty decent, however there are always exceptions; there are men who managed to make me feel like a nasty crack whore, leaving bruises all over my body or grabbing my hair telling me to take it down the throat and I'd better swallow what they gave cuz they're paying good money and this goes on and on and soon they become a blur of faces; the only way I could stand it was the thought of smoking a big rock and to keep smoking it until everything faded away.

LOVE VI

Kayla was much older than me I wasn't even twenty years old and I never had a relationship before and so maybe she was the blueprint for all those future hookups and I feel so disappointed that I can't look back with appreciation for her, for providing me with definitions of what love was, and it was a textbook case for domestic violence and still I stayed because I never felt that way for someone before; in the beginning love was full of nervous energy and urges to touch and bashful glances and it soon developed into endless desire and urges to please and to look after what had become mine, but drugs poison everything so the demons came out to play and twist what we had come to share, tempers became short and scary fights repeated as frustration spilled over and we were bouncing from place to place sometimes getting kicked out sometimes sleeping on the SkyTrain to rest somewhere safe and that first moment of violence as Kayla threw a CD right at my face, she was so sorry she didn't mean to and it was forgiven but it became usual and expected like how she controlled whatever I did and how I got so dependent on her for drugs that the violent outbursts were worth it and soon I was a cash cow and that was that, I hit bottom; when everything changed I hid the part of me that escaped her anger, kept this part of my soul safe, safe from a lover who'd broken me into pieces.

RUSH

At least part of the rush was the construction of the crack pipe: my heart beat so fast as I crumpled the Brillo into a ball and heated it up and crunched into the stem and fit the small plastic hose onto the pipe, placed the rock in and lit up; Kayla would snake a long hose up her sleeve that came out her collar and she'd do a toke on the SkyTrain or the bus or even while she walked down the street and often smoked a cigarette at the same time to disguise the smoke, she used a torch lighter and burned the rock in a way that got you high as a kite and sometimes after such a hit she would think the cops were coming and stuff her pockets with her dog's ashes, with cigarettes, with her ID or whatever she thought was important to go to jail with, you could call her an expert when it came to the mechanics of using drugs and though she taught me I was only able to replicate her heart-busting tokes a few times.

PAY PHONE

I was gone for too long so Kayla smacked my head against a pay phone, she'd told a drug dealer that I'd blow him for crack however a few minutes in he started getting phone calls from clients wanting to buy dope so I rode shotgun with him while he delivered drugs all over town and it was a relief to spend time away from her as I felt like she was drowning me; one of the ways we would keep in contact while we roamed around town was that she would whistle very loudly and I'd go to that location, however as I was dropped off this time I could see she was very angry but the violence of having my forehead smashed into the pay phone was something I was not expecting even though she often put her hands on me, I don't know why I kept coming back and I don't know why she didn't leave me if I angered her so badly though I think we were tied to each other, she felt responsible for me and I felt dependent on her, it was running not on love and respect but on money and dope, she was my first girlfriend.

BUNK

The emotion you feel when someone bunks you is the worst feeling of frustration and anger, the times I was bunked with wax instead of crack made me feel murderous and if I had the guts I'd beat the crap out of whoever ripped me off, there is this energy in finding money and then trying to find a dealer, and in those moments of craving is when some asshole decides to give you crap instead of crack, when you get too dope-simple and trust whoever says they have rock to sell, and it's your own fault for trusting people, it's wise not to trust those who ride on bikes as it's easy for them to bunk you and wheel away right quick but personally I'd be too afraid to go around ripping people off because that puts a big target on your back and you will eventually get caught and who knows what will happen then.

DOMESTIC

I was afraid he would hit my friend the wrong way and kill her cuz he'd already stabbed her with a metal push stick and broke her glasses, one time after arguing with him he snuck up behind us and pushed her against the wall, while she protested for him to leave her alone, two construction men were watching and I was afraid to step in and get hurt but he forcibly kissed her and left, after that we sat on the bench and smoked rock, I listened to her talk about her boyfriend and how she loved him and I thought to myself how I ignored those first signs of violence like the moment Kayla threw a CD at me which made us go silent with shock and then how laughter followed, as time went by her anger progressed but there were loving moments after the violence as she apologized for hurting me and it's these moments that made me stay but I was also afraid that she would go too far and that I would die at the hands of someone I loved.

LOVE VII

I was cold and tired and had just fought with Kayla so I convinced a taxi driver to drive me home, my mom paid him, the area of town we were hanging at was Kingsway near Slocan and we got separated after a typical scrap so I decided to fuck it and just see if I could go home to my parents, I was tired of being stressed and bullied and sold on the street and letting myself be treated this way, what was wrong with me, so I slept and then woke up to Kayla in the backyard asking to speak to me, so I went out and she said how much she loved me and needed me and wanted me by her side and I fell for it hook, line and sinker, when we were good together it was great and we were a team, we made intense love but when it was bad there was so much anger between us that sometimes it came out as violence and humiliation yet we always ended up back together no matter that there seemed to be no respect left, the last time I saw her before I was arrested she made me sit on a backpack in front of her on the ground so she could keep an eye on me but I had enough so I left and fell asleep on a bench in a park and in the morning she left my backpack at a Western Union with the message that she would be downtown yet I wouldn't see her until a couple years later, I truly believe that if I wasn't arrested I would have died either by a trick or an overdose or even by Kayla cuz she was so much stronger than me and expressed her anger by raising her hand to me, that time between the first time I used and the time that I was arrested was one long downward spiral where I lost weight and self-respect and probably almost my life.

Part Three

WITNESS

The DTES is full of Asians working and living their lives, I also think they're an audience to the tragic comedy of skid row's drunks and addicts, Hastings is like a fishbowl unaware of the outside, like a world unto itself, the residents of Chinatown watch the show while selling herbs and ducks and doing their daily, once I started noticing it I saw watchers everywhere like older men walking with their hands behind their backs looking at deals being done or addicts huddled against buildings smoking dope, on Cordova Street groups of Asians have their work breaks and smoke their cigarettes and watch the busy business of street traffic, they're mostly silent watchers as I've never had an Asian resident of Chinatown or the DTES bother me or tell me to fuck off, it's just a consistent surveying; though I mostly ignored them, sometimes I became angry like when this one man kept staring at me, he would walk by blatantly eyeballing me and when I complained to my friend he pushed the dude to get him to keep going, overall though I really don't mind because with all the bullshit that goes on in the streets it might as well be a reality show.

HIGH

Sometimes people act very strangely when they're high, this one woman was nodding out while standing on the sidewalk drooling and then she took off her shirt and shuffled around half-naked, of course the cops came rather quick for that one, another woman would do a toke and then twirl around all over in circles obviously orbiting the moons of Jupiter and taking over space on the sidewalk, one woman would smoke and her eyes would bulge out of her head and she'd go silent, not making a sound, while looking around like she'd lost her marbles, every time when I saw a junkie nod out I couldn't help but worry that they'd crack their heads open, my one friend would inject a big hit of coke and heroin which caused her to nod until her face was at her knees however she never fell even though I was sure she would, what grinds my teeth about guys getting high is that sometimes they would get aroused, like this one man who got a raging hard-on every time he smoked rock and would fondle himself with this stupid look on his face; when I got high I was no better as I'd get quiet and think there were small cameras on the TV or a stereo that were recording everything and I'd get leery about who I was with, everyone has their own way of experiencing a high and sometimes it's totally wacky or annoying or downright scary.

DEALER

I tried dealing a couple times and failed miserably cuz to deal one has to be able to capture the attention of people walking by and have an ability to hustle and negotiate and be tough enough not to get bullied; I have a hard time yelling or talking loudly so imagine me trying to sell to people especially with the stress of dealing under the watchful eyes of the man, once I was ten dollars short and got smacked in the face a couple times, it's like being cuffed to the person you're working for cuz you owe the dope you took to sell, it's a way of making money so a lot of people do it but I'm glad I quit while I was ahead before I started owing a lot of money which is never a good thing, people get in trouble when they owe especially if a debt collector is sent after them which is scary, like once I watched a collector get creative and put together different types of weapons which was pretty clever-looking and ominous, this system works for you and you can double your money but either way it's vicious.

NATIVE

I've seen so many down-and-out Native people, it hurt my heart to see them drinking Listerine and cheap wine, constantly drunk and red-faced; as an Aboriginal I have to admit it shamed me that I had become another statistic as if I proved to racists that Natives were just alcoholic drug addicts, we have feelings and loved ones and stories and struggles and fears, we are people and we have dreams, people see rough-looking men and women swaying while walking maybe talking to themselves and smelling like shit and see only the outside, I saw myself as a stereotype going around smoking crack and drinking and not respecting my body or mind and forgetting the power of my culture, I see generations of dysfunction and trauma, souls destroying themselves through drink and crack and heroin and how people turn away not wanting to look.

THEFT

I couldn't believe it that Kayla managed to steal a DVD player from the mall, me and my friend were at the edge of the parking lot when we saw her running toward us with a big box in her hands and no one was trying to catch her and so we sold that for drugs, a lot of addicts are damn thieves and will steal stuff to sell or trade and Kim was an expert at it, she often used small copper pipe fittings and a long hose to make crack pipes and you find this stuff at places like Rona where she often stole the pieces she needed, there are also those shitheads who ride around on bikes with bolt cutters in their backpacks looking for places to break in or when you're grinding for dope and stupidly give your money to a middleman and they disappear; the only time I ever stole was my sister's cellphone which I sold for a measly twenty bucks and boy did I feel bad afterward because stealing kind of rubs me the wrong way but there are people who would sell their own grandmothers for some rock, one thing I never did was steal someone else's drugs because if you are found out prepare for a sustained beating or worse so going down the path of the thief is something I would not recommend.

FEMALES

Women really do get the shit end of the stick, women do what they have to do to survive in a world where men exploit them and control them and rape them and kill them, men use drugs like a carrot on a stick to lure women into trading their bodies for a high, for cash, women turn hard to deal with the ruthlessness of the streets and many take advantage of each other, women are humiliated and hurt and cuz the area is small they run into their rapists on the block or in rehab or needle exchanges, young girls get turned out to endless tricks while being forcibly confined to some scummy, scary hotel room by pimps, one woman told me not to do this trick cuz he tended to degrade but she needed the money which was only twenty dollars and she would give me a few rocks so I stayed in the bathroom while he took advantage of her desperation and sodomized her, there was this other woman who was a predator herself and often resorted to violence to intimidate and collect, now as much as women fuck each other over I blame the men for an environment where exploitation and violence thrive.

VERMIN, BUGS AND BIRDS

The rats that populate the DTES are big and fat, the back alleys are their playground and they're not afraid to go right up to people while they're smoking rock or shooting up smack, sometimes when I got stuck in the alley after doing drugs I sat on some stairs so still that the rats would come out and scuttle around my legs and I would fear that I would get eaten alive, once this girl let me stay in her room for a bit and soon I heard noises deep inside her pile of clothes and this little mouse peeked through and looked at me, I swear the pigeons get high on all the dropped crack cuz they spend all day picking the ground at the feet of addicts and dealers and fly over alleys crapping on people's heads; now bed bugs and cockroaches are what I hate the most, I'd be sitting in a room and the walls would start crawling and I'd see roaches in the sink and on the floor which would make me feel itchy and out of there I would go, bed bugs are even worse those little fuckers will find a way to infest all the corners and radios and beds and sheets of a room, these things are the wildlife of skid row, surviving on garbage and leftovers.

HEALTH

As my drug use continued to rise my health began to fail, in the beginning the meth that I was doing leaked out of my pores and caused the first rumblings of drug psychosis, it didn't help that the woman I was doing crystal with thought there were aliens and cameras everywhere, soon I lost a lot of weight as I often forgot to eat and when I did it was fast food and as I began to smoke crack I had twigs for legs and my hip bones jutted out and I became dehydrated from not drinking enough water, for a long time I didn't brush my teeth and they became yellow from doing drugs and eating junk food and smoking cigarettes, an abscess infected part of my neck coming up the side of my face and I had tiny cuts on my hands from the Brillo and it felt like I was hacking up my lungs every morning, I was weak and my brain cells were getting killed, I was becoming slow from all that dope, I would stay up for days and become paranoid about everything; it took jail to recover my mind and body, I had to get locked up to save my life.

HOSPITAL

I ended up in the hospital for different reasons, one time I woke up at St. Paul's being warmed with blankets, I freaked out cuz I thought I was being assaulted so they kicked me out and I passed out across the street and was later thrown in the drunk tank, another is when I was deep in a cocaine psychosis, digging a hole and acting bizarre and someone called the ambulance on me and I spent my time verbally abusing the hospital staff, I got knocked out once and the blood was all over the place but I was okay and they released me, before going to youth detox I cut a large hole in my arm and at the hospital told them I fell on a nail of course they knew that was bullshit, after a stupid fight with Kayla I overdosed on Aspirin and spent sixteen days in the psych ward where my parents would visit me and bring burgers and during one of their visits I puked my guts out after swallowing the charcoal and trying to eat the KFC my parents brought me; that was the longest time I was ever in the hospital and almost every hour they took blood until my veins were shot and the nurse burst the vein in my hand and it turned into a bubble, my mother said she would never forget the look on the doctor's face.

HOPE

I know what it's like to have no hope though I felt no emotion about selling myself when I was high, the self-hatred I had when I was sober ate me alive and could only be blocked out by the constant use of crack cocaine which was my drug of choice and no matter if I was cold or hungry or thirsty, making money for rock always came first, it came before family before my self-respect before food before friendship before love, before life—hope had no place in the life I was living and the only thing I looked forward to was my next toke, I would sit on the stairs in the alley so high I was unable to get up and I'd see the rats and shit and garbage and needles and I would briefly wonder if life was worth living and if this is what it all came down to; when it came to love I thought I found it and that we would live happily ever after and that she was my hope for something better but instead everything grew worse until I couldn't breathe or talk or do anything unless I had permission; during those early times I was rarely sober but when I was clean for a day or two I felt so empty it was like I turned into a skeleton with no guts or heart just a mouth to smoke crack.

DRYING OUT

Instead of procuring drugs in jail I used the time to become sober, soon I started to care about things that I had not cared about for a while like drinking coffee or having a good night's sleep or eating regularly but the biggest thing I wanted was to connect with another human, like I began to want to be liked and to be desired and to have a friendship not based on drugs but it took a long time for the psychosis to go away; I would be in my living space and think strange things and what's funny was the paranoia over being watched cuz it was true, we were all being watched through cameras and guards, jail was all about routine and soon I was getting pretty bored so I chased tail and had a few girlfriends on the side which filled a need to be loved whether it was real or not, it was like ice thawing and I had to face the type of person I was, that I took advantage of people and people took advantage of me and I did whatever I had to do to get that rock and slowly the layers peeled away and what was left was a broken woman taking notice of life again.

NEVER ENDING

One time when I tried leaving downtown I failed, every time I
walked a couple blocks a regular would show up in a car and stop
to talk to me, I would find a dealer and with the money I had just
earned, buy rock, get high, when I became unstuck and started to
walk away, another regular would stop by me and the whole thing
would happen again, I was so tired, the sun would rise and set and
the night would come and the people would venture out and the
same old bullshit would happen, there were men who would pick
up different women multiple times, I would see them in their cars
driving down Hastings then turning around and going through back
alleys and side streets, I'd go two steps and one of these guys would
stop me and I'd still be so high I ignored my exhaustion.

TRIGGERS

Using dreams are so real and so frustrating, the entire dream is one complicated mission to find drugs and when I finally come across them, I wake up without smoking the rock and so I'm lying in bed feeling like I got bunked or something, smell can be a trigger too like burning wax or plastic cuz it smells like crack smoke or the hose on the end of a pipe, alleys that stink of garbage and urine and shit often make me think of being too high and getting stuck by the Dumpsters smoking rock after rock, I had roamed all over Vancouver and North Vancouver and Maple Ridge and so some locations are triggers like the Downtown Eastside where just being there gives me cravings and makes me nervous that I'll meet a person I know and get sucked back into that lifestyle cuz I am susceptible to persuasion, even nighttime can trigger cravings as the night makes me excited to go out and wander the streets doing what I want and doing drugs or drinking and having no plans and not knowing where I'll end up; for so long I used drugs to deal with anything that caused stress like turning tricks or coping with domestic abuse or the energy it took to get dope or the anxiety of not having a stable place to live and so stress is a trigger too since I used drugs to forget about it and now in my sober life I have to live with these things that make my life a little complicated.

DETOX

Mad respect to the workers on the front line in the youth detoxes in Vancouver, they took me in when I called at my worst and gave me food, board, safety and most importantly a break from the drug life and there was no judging only what could be done to make it easier—one time I was barely there, nodding out during the whole processing part and I sat in detox trying to sip chicken soup, almost falling out of my chair, the detox was in a big house and we had our own rooms and there was a kitchen and big meals and a TV and books and crafts, it was a very safe place and even though I'd be clean for seven days, or leave early, I was still treated with respect and they were still proud if I only had a few days clean—there were the candy people too who walked around handing out candy and the street nurses and the van that distributed rigs and condoms and juice and passed along info to women on bad dates.

SHADOWS

Once when I was sober for a good amount of time I had to face memories that began to bubble to the surface, I thought to myself *how could I have done the things I've done* but I also thought these were just memories so they didn't bother me, it was one big fucking contradiction; chasing rock is full-time business and it's easy to get lost along the way and it's easy to get into trouble and it is definitely easy to get hurt so why do it? I did it to get fucking high and getting high helped to ignore memories of shit I did to get ripped so I guess I have mixed feelings about the trash that comes with drug addiction; I think back and marvel at the danger I put myself in over and over again for that moment of being high and how I have to live with that for the rest of my life; I will always have those memories and that blur of men's faces, their shadows that follow me quietly.

UPSTANDING CITIZEN

Once I was sitting on the curb with a couple people and after looking around I took a toke from my pipe and when I exhaled I looked up and saw the cops watching me from their car and I felt like I almost had a heart attack but they rolled on flashing lights to tell us to move on which completely ruined my high and I was fucked for the next ten minutes; sober now I still feel a soft, slight twitch whenever I see a cop car cuz for years while using on the street I'd been looking out for patrollers until it became second nature and I'd make a hole in the bottom hem of my hoodie that I could stick my rock and pipe into in case they decided to frisk for whatever reason; this mindset is slowly going away cuz I have no reason to be fearful of the police anymore and I have nothing to hide from no one, it's like I turned into an upstanding citizen not breaking the law no more.

CLEAN

I've had so much excitement, if you can call it that, in my life that I won't mind if the rest of my years are simple and quiet, I love that first coffee in the morning while reading a book, my writing, taking the dogs for a walk, being relaxed; I've become pretty good at blocking things from my mind so I don't go crazy from the dysfunction and fear and endless cravings.

DIFFERENCES

I'm not the same as I used to be, I'm more stupid and slow now and I need things explained to me more than once, I'm not saying I'm dumb, I'm saying all the crack I smoked killed a shitload of my brain cells and I need a little more help than I used to, I also feel that I'm more anxious than I ever was and this makes me more afraid of things and more afraid over shit that shouldn't be feared, I'm a nervous Nelly and this anxiety burns my nerves right up.

STREETS

It may sound very stupid but there's something about the streets that always appealed to me, there was a type of freedom where I could do what I wanted when I wanted wherever I wanted and never be tied down to one place, the only rules being those of the street, never staying in one place for long, on an endless journey for more and more drugs until it became the most important task at hand and I could not plan anything because I didn't know where I would be in any foreseeable future and I had no address, however the flip side to all this was that I was tied up—I was a prisoner and everything that came with it, I was a coin, each side a cell with thick bars.

NOTES

"xxx" and "Shadows" have been published in *Sex Worker Wisdom*, edited by Amber Dawn for the PACE society.

"Lonely Men," "Maple Ridge" and "Love 1" are forthcoming in *Hustling Verse* edited by Amber Dawn and Justin Ducharme, and published by Arsenal Pulp Press.

ACKNOWLEDGEMENTS

I would like to thank my editor Amber McMillan and Nightwood Editions for taking a chance and believing in this book. I would like to thank my friends for their support and feedback. I thank my family for sticking by me and loving me through thick and thin. A special thanks to Amber Dawn who has supported me since the beginning. I also acknowledge the women I have met on the streets, whose stories are important and whose lives are meaningful. Mussi Cho. Thank you.

ABOUT THE AUTHOR

Cassandra Blanchard was born in Whitehorse, Yukon, and is part of the Selkirk First Nation. She attended the University of British Columbia and recently received a Bachelor of Arts. *Fresh Pack of Smokes* is her first book. She currently lives on Vancouver Island.